Property of ....

GUN COLLECTOR'S LOGBOOK

GUN COLLECTOR'S LOGBOOK

Track Your
ACQUISITIONS, REPAIRS, AND SALES

chartwell
books

Contents

Introduction

Gun Collector's Logbook is intended to provide a convenient source for firearms collectors, hunters, trap shooters, and other sporting enthusiasts to keep an orderly record of their collection. In addition to descriptive information that will aid in identifying and appraising each firearm, the terms in the log pages correspond to the language required by the Bureau of Alcohol, Tobacco, Firearms and Explosives regulations 27 CFR Part 478 for legal acquisition and disposition. The book is divided into three sections, Rifles, Shotguns, and Handguns, which are generally considered to be the three main types of firearms.

DESCRIPTION NOTES

Whether you're new to gun ownership or you're transferring data from notebooks or other loose records, you may wish to add rich descriptive and personal notes of each firearm to aid in the understanding and enjoyment of your collection. You may fill them in however you wish, but depending on the type of firearm you have, they could include the following descriptions:

Action	bolt, lever, hinge or break open, pump, semi-auto, auto-loader; single-action, double-action, muzzleloader
Gauge	12-gauge, 16-gauge, 20-gauge; 3-inch
Caliber	.45, .357, 9-mm
Choke	full, modified, improved
Barrel	single or double; side-by-side, over-under; length in inches
Finish	bluing, parkerized, nickel, chrome, stainless; plating, refinished, restored
Grips	walnut, rubber, ivory, polymer, fiberglass; target grip
Stock	width, texture; wood, fiberglass; 1-piece, 2-piece, full stock, fore-end, cheekpiece
Sights	iron, front-fixed/rear-adjustable, peep, laser, bead
Scope	crosshair, red dot, telescopic, reflex
Condition	new, perfect or "as new," excellent, very good, good, fair
Other Characteristics, Special Marks & Accessories	anything that's important to you, such as family history or historical significance of the piece; other things that come with it such as case or spare magazine; any unique marks
Maintenance Records, Modifications, Photo, or Receipt	refurbishing or replacement parts; cleaning quirks; refinishing, customization, or engraving

VALUATION AND SALES

Determining the current value of a gun will aid in the purchasing or selling of it for a fair price. It's also helpful information for heirs who may need to liquidate a collection. There are a number of books and resources that estimate firearm values.

The Blue Book of Gun Values by Steve Fjestad is among the most-used pricing guides. Updated yearly, it is comprehensive and extensive. It uses the Photo Percentage Grading System (PPGS), a standardized firearms grading system that relies on percentages of original finish(es) to ascertain the correct grade of each gun's unique condition. It includes full-color reference photos with thorough descriptions, and it has an online subscription feature. The guide's drawback is that it cannot be used to evaluate a gun that's been refinished.

Another useful source is *Standard Catalog of Firearms*. Frequently updated, this comprehensive guide includes photos and pricing for nearly every rifle, shotgun, and handgun made or sold since the 1800s. The latest edition uses the NRA's rating system for antique firearm pricing (pre-1899).

Additionally, there are valuation books for military firearms; air guns and black powder guns; and individual manufacturers such as Smith & Wesson, Winchester, Colt, Remington, Luger, etc. Websites such as GunBroker.com and GunsAmerica.com, as well as magazines such as *GunDigest*, offer listings of guns for sale so you can compare similar models in similar conditions. The NRA Museum (nramuseum.org) has more suggestions on how to research firearms values, specifically antiques.

In general, these are the considerations that will aid in making an estimate of the value of a gun:

Identification
Primarily make (manufacturer) and model, but also variation and sub-variations such as barrel length, unusual finish or markings, or special configurations. To positively impact value, any deviations from the standard must be factory original, not later modifications. The make and model name will be easy to identify on most modern firearms, but older or antique guns may have limited markings; in this case, consulting other collectors and reference books can be helpful in identifying the gun.

Condition

Accurately assessing a gun's condition is critical in determining its value. As noted above, the *Blue Book of Gun Values* relies on estimating how much of the original finish remains on the gun. Another widely use method for describing condition is the NRA Firearms Condition Standards (nramuseum.org), which employs different definitions for modern and antique firearms. These range from New to Fair (for modern) and from Factory New to Poor (for antique).

Special considerations

Take into consideration any alterations that could reduce a gun's value, such as refinishing, replacing parts, or any embellishments, such as engravings, that were poorly done. Things that might boost value include customization and historical or decorative engravings.

For acquisition and disposition of any firearms, it's crucial that you track where your guns came from and where they're going. Record the name and address or name and license number of the person you are buying from or selling to. Rules and regulations for the sale and transfer of modern firearms differ from antique (curios and relics), so it's imperative to consult *Federal Firearms Regulations Reference Guide* (atf.gov).

SAFETY CONSIDERATIONS

Safety is the foundation of responsible gun ownership. The number one rule among many organizations and enthusiasts alike, whether using, cleaning, or storing, is to *treat all guns as if they are loaded.* Further, the National Rifle Association (NRA) and the National Shooting Sports Foundation (NSSF) outline these fundamental gun safety rules:

1. Always point the gun in a safe direction. Never point it in a direction, including while loading, that you do not intend to shoot.

2. Always keep your finger off the trigger until you are ready to shoot. Do not rely on the safety!

3. Always keep the gun unloaded when not in use. Never assume a gun is unloaded.

4. Know your target and what's beyond it. Think first. Shoot second.

5. Know how to use the gun safely. Know its basic parts and learn how it operates, including how to load and unload ammunition. Learn the proper way to carry and handle each type of gun safely.

6. Be sure the gun is safe to operate. General upkeep, such as regular cleaning and proper storage, are essential for your gun to operate correctly and safely. (It will also help extend its life and maintain its value.) Make sure there are no obstructions in the barrel and that there is no ammunition in the chamber before use.

7. Use the correct ammunition for your gun. Most guns have the ammunition type (BBs, pellets, shells, cartridges) stamped on the barrel. You can also refer to your owner's manual.

8. Wear safety glass and earmuffs or ear plugs when shooting. It's also a good idea to wear eye protection when cleaning your gun. Keep in mind that many shooting activities and certain types of guns require additional safety precautions.

9. Store guns so they are not accessible to unauthorized people. A gun's safety is no substitute! Teach kids what to do if they find a gun: Stop! Don't touch. Run away. Tell a grown-up (eddieeagle.nra.org).

10. Never use alcohol, drugs, or certain medications that can cause physical or mental impairment while handling your gun.

11. A clean gun is a safe gun. Clean after every use as well as after prolonged storage. Make sure the gun is unloaded, and the action open, during cleaning. Service your gun regularly, according to manufacturer's recommendations, and do not make alterations or modifications to any gun.

Rifles

A weapon designed or redesigned, made or remade, and intended to be fired from the shoulder, and designed or redesigned and made or remade to use the energy of an explosive to fire only a single projectile through a rifled bore for each single pull of the trigger.

~ 26 U.S.C. Chapter 53 §5845(c)

Make	
Model Name/Number	
Serial Number	
Manufacturer/Importer	
Caliber	
Capacity	
Action	
Barrel Length	
Finish	
Stock/Fore-end	
Sights	
Scope	
Condition	

Other Characteristics, Special Marks & Accessories

_____

_____

_____

_____

_____

Date Purchased	
From (name/address or license no.)	
Price	

Date Sold	
To (name/address or license no.)	
Price	

Current/Replacement Value	
Insured	

Maintenance Records, Modifications, Photo, or Receipt

_____

_____

_____

_____

_____

_____

_____

Make	
Model Name/Number	
Serial Number	
Manufacturer/Importer	
Caliber	
Capacity	
Action	
Barrel Length	
Finish	
Stock/Fore-end	
Sights	
Scope	
Condition	

Other Characteristics, Special Marks & Accessories

_____

_____

_____

_____

_____

Date Purchased	
From (name/address or license no.)	
Price	

Date Sold	
To (name/address or license no.)	
Price	

Current/Replacement Value	
Insured	

Maintenance Records, Modifications, Photo, or Receipt

_____

_____

_____

_____

_____

_____

_____

Make	
Model Name/Number	
Serial Number	
Manufacturer/Importer	
Caliber	
Capacity	
Action	
Barrel Length	
Finish	
Stock/Fore-end	
Sights	
Scope	
Condition	

Other Characteristics, Special Marks & Accessories

_____

_____

_____

_____

_____

Date Purchased	
From (name/address or license no.)	
Price	

Date Sold	
To (name/address or license no.)	
Price	

Current/Replacement Value	
Insured	

Maintenance Records, Modifications, Photo, or Receipt

_____

_____

_____

_____

_____

_____

Make	
Model Name/Number	
Serial Number	
Manufacturer/Importer	
Caliber	
Capacity	
Action	
Barrel Length	
Finish	
Stock/Fore-end	
Sights	
Scope	
Condition	

Other Characteristics, Special Marks & Accessories

_____

_____

_____

_____

_____

Date Purchased	
From (name/address or license no.)	
Price	

Date Sold	
To (name/address or license no.)	
Price	

Current/Replacement Value	
Insured	

Maintenance Records, Modifications, Photo, or Receipt

_____

_____

_____

_____

_____

_____

_____

Popular Firearms of Western Gunslingers

In *The Good, the Bad, and the Ugly* (1966), Clint Eastwood's Man with No Name used a Winchester 1866 "Yellow Boy" with a side folding scope. Though this particular model wasn't quite right for the time period, it was made to look like the Henry 1860, which was more appropriate, by removing the wooden forend.

In *Unforgiven* (1992), Morgan Freeman's Ned Logan uses a Spencer 1860 Carbine, claiming that with it, he could shoot a flying bird in the eye. This particular model had a saddle ring, which allowed it to be tied to a saddle. Interestingly, the costar and director of the film, Clint Eastwood, uses the gun later in the movie. (It was also a gun used by his character in *The Good, the Bad, and the Ugly*.)

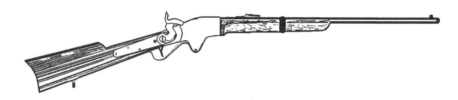

John Wayne, the original film cowboy, used a Winchester Model 1892 in a dozen films, first appearing in *Stagecoach* (1939). Because of the Duke, this model was associated with the Hollywood western for decades. But even more than the Winchester, Wayne's Colt 1873 Single Action Army Revolver appeared in twice that many films, from 1931 to 1976. It's noteworthy that both models could have used the same cartridge, a convenience that cowboys at the time would have appreciated.

The Lone Ranger's (1952–54) masked hero used a Colt .45 single-action revolver. The well-recognized firearm used by John Hart's ranger had an ivory grip and intricate engravings. The same type of weapon was used by Wyatt Earp in the famous shootout at the O.K. Corral in Tombstone, Arizona, in 1881.

Make	
Model Name/Number	
Serial Number	
Manufacturer/Importer	
Caliber	
Capacity	
Action	
Barrel Length	
Finish	
Stock/Fore-end	
Sights	
Scope	
Condition	

Other Characteristics, Special Marks & Accessories

_____

_____

_____

_____

_____

Date Purchased	
From (name/address or license no.)	
Price	

Date Sold	
To (name/address or license no.)	
Price	

Current/Replacement Value	
Insured	

Maintenance Records, Modifications, Photo, or Receipt

_____

_____

_____

_____

_____

_____

_____

Make	
Model Name/Number	
Serial Number	
Manufacturer/Importer	
Caliber	
Capacity	
Action	
Barrel Length	
Finish	
Stock/Fore-end	
Sights	
Scope	
Condition	

Other Characteristics, Special Marks & Accessories

_____

_____

_____

_____

_____

Date Purchased	
From (name/address or license no.)	
Price	

Date Sold	
To (name/address or license no.)	
Price	

Current/Replacement Value	
Insured	

Maintenance Records, Modifications, Photo, or Receipt

_____

_____

_____

_____

_____

_____

Make	
Model Name/Number	
Serial Number	
Manufacturer/Importer	
Caliber	
Capacity	
Action	
Barrel Length	
Finish	
Stock/Fore-end	
Sights	
Scope	
Condition	

Other Characteristics, Special Marks & Accessories

_____

_____

_____

_____

_____

Date Purchased	
From (name/address or license no.)	
Price	

Date Sold	
To (name/address or license no.)	
Price	

Current/Replacement Value	
Insured	

Maintenance Records, Modifications, Photo, or Receipt

_____

_____

_____

_____

_____

_____

_____

Make	
Model Name/Number	
Serial Number	
Manufacturer/Importer	
Caliber	
Capacity	
Action	
Barrel Length	
Finish	
Stock/Fore-end	
Sights	
Scope	
Condition	

Other Characteristics, Special Marks & Accessories

_____

_____

_____

_____

_____

Date Purchased	
From (name/address or license no.)	
Price	

Date Sold	
To (name/address or license no.)	
Price	

Current/Replacement Value	
Insured	

Maintenance Records, Modifications, Photo, or Receipt

_____

_____

_____

_____

_____

_____

_____

Historical Timeline of Firearms
(1288–1750)

| 1288 | The oldest surviving firearm, or Heilongjiang "hand cannon," was 14 inches long and made from bronze, and it used gunpowder alchemy that had already been in use in China for centuries. |

| 1364 | The first recorded use of a firearm, fired when powder inside the barrel was ignited by holding a burning wick to a "touch hole." |

| 1411 | The matchlock gun appears in Europe, utilizing the first lock and flash pan for mechanically firing a gun, which improved aim. |

| 1498 | The rifling principle is discovered. These spiral grooves etched inside a gun's barrel help impart a spinning motion to a bullet when fired, making it more stable and accurate. |

| 1509 | The wheel lock is invented, which generates a spark mechanically (rather than keeping a wick lit), making it easier and more reliable to use. |

1500s	Fowling pieces, long-barreled smoothbore firearms used to hunt low-flying birds, are developed; they become fashionable among the upper classes in the late 1700s.
late 1500s	A lid is added to the flash pan, to protect the powder from the elements, but it has to be moved manually.
1610	Marin le Bourgeois develops the first flintlock for King Louis XIII of France. Known as the "French lock," the trigger releases a springed mechanism that causes a frizzen to strike a flint; the resulting spark ignites gunpowder and propels a ball (bullet).
1630	The flintlock, by now standardly designed to push back the lid and spark a flint at the same time, becomes the main weapon of European armies until it's replaced by the percussion lock.

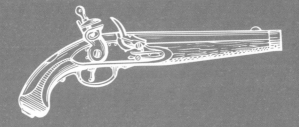

1637	First use of proof marks to show the nationality of the gun's manufacturer.
1750	Dueling pistols become en vogue over rapiers.

Make	
Model Name/Number	
Serial Number	
Manufacturer/Importer	
Caliber	
Capacity	
Action	
Barrel Length	
Finish	
Stock/Fore-end	
Sights	
Scope	
Condition	

Other Characteristics, Special Marks & Accessories

_____

_____

_____

_____

_____

Date Purchased	
From (name/address or license no.)	
Price	

Date Sold	
To (name/address or license no.)	
Price	

Current/Replacement Value	
Insured	

Maintenance Records, Modifications, Photo, or Receipt

_____

_____

_____

_____

_____

_____

_____

Make	
Model Name/Number	
Serial Number	
Manufacturer/Importer	
Caliber	
Capacity	
Action	
Barrel Length	
Finish	
Stock/Fore-end	
Sights	
Scope	
Condition	

Other Characteristics, Special Marks & Accessories

_____

_____

_____

_____

_____

Date Purchased	
From (name/address or license no.)	
Price	

Date Sold	
To (name/address or license no.)	
Price	

Current/Replacement Value	
Insured	

Maintenance Records, Modifications, Photo, or Receipt

_____

_____

_____

_____

_____

_____

Make	
Model Name/Number	
Serial Number	
Manufacturer/Importer	
Caliber	
Capacity	
Action	
Barrel Length	
Finish	
Stock/Fore-end	
Sights	
Scope	
Condition	

Other Characteristics, Special Marks & Accessories

_____

_____

_____

_____

_____

Date Purchased	
From (name/address or license no.)	
Price	

Date Sold	
To (name/address or license no.)	
Price	

Current/Replacement Value	
Insured	

Maintenance Records, Modifications, Photo, or Receipt

_____

_____

_____

_____

_____

_____

_____

Make	
Model Name/Number	
Serial Number	
Manufacturer/Importer	
Caliber	
Capacity	
Action	
Barrel Length	
Finish	
Stock/Fore-end	
Sights	
Scope	
Condition	

Other Characteristics, Special Marks & Accessories

_____

_____

_____

_____

_____

Date Purchased	
From (name/address or license no.)	
Price	

Date Sold	
To (name/address or license no.)	
Price	

Current/Replacement Value	
Insured	

Maintenance Records, Modifications, Photo, or Receipt

_____

_____

_____

_____

_____

_____

_____

The World's Largest Collection

The J.M. Davis Arms & Historical Museum in Claremore, Oklahoma, is the world's largest privately held collection of firearms. It houses more than 12,000 firearms and thousands of non-firearm artifacts, from Old West saddles to World War I posters. It is said that John Monroe Davis was set on this path when his father bribed the youngster to take his medicine by giving him a small muzzleloading shotgun.

Davis served as mayor of Claremore from 1921 to 1923 and from 1933 to 1943, during which time he met Will Rogers. Though many museums, including the Smithsonian Institution, attempted to purchase all or part of the collection, Davis wanted it to remain in its entirety in Claremore. In 1965, he established a nonprofit foundation to become the collection's owner, which then leased it to the State of Oklahoma for 99 years (for the cost of $1). That same year, the governor appropriated funds to purchase an entire city block, where the museum opened in 1969 and still stands.

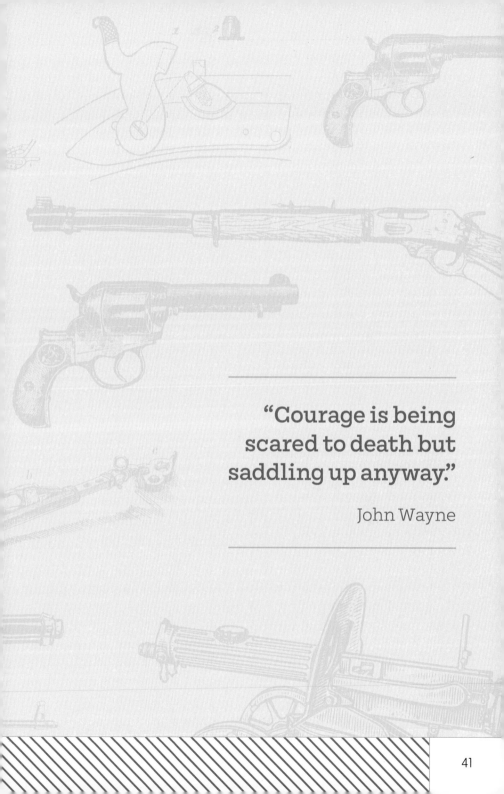

"Courage is being scared to death but saddling up anyway."

John Wayne

Make	
Model Name/Number	
Serial Number	
Manufacturer/Importer	
Caliber	
Capacity	
Action	
Barrel Length	
Finish	
Stock/Fore-end	
Sights	
Scope	
Condition	

Other Characteristics, Special Marks & Accessories

_____

_____

_____

_____

_____

Date Purchased	
From (name/address or license no.)	
Price	

Date Sold	
To (name/address or license no.)	
Price	

Current/Replacement Value	
Insured	

Maintenance Records, Modifications, Photo, or Receipt

_____

_____

_____

_____

_____

_____

_____

Make	
Model Name/Number	
Serial Number	
Manufacturer/Importer	
Caliber	
Capacity	
Action	
Barrel Length	
Finish	
Stock/Fore-end	
Sights	
Scope	
Condition	

Other Characteristics, Special Marks & Accessories

_____

_____

_____

_____

_____

Date Purchased	
From (name/address or license no.)	
Price	

Date Sold	
To (name/address or license no.)	
Price	

Current/Replacement Value	
Insured	

Maintenance Records, Modifications, Photo, or Receipt

_____

_____

_____

_____

_____

_____

_____

Make	
Model Name/Number	
Serial Number	
Manufacturer/Importer	
Caliber	
Capacity	
Action	
Barrel Length	
Finish	
Stock/Fore-end	
Sights	
Scope	
Condition	

Other Characteristics, Special Marks & Accessories

_____

_____

_____

_____

_____

Date Purchased	
From (name/address or license no.)	
Price	

Date Sold	
To (name/address or license no.)	
Price	

Current/Replacement Value	
Insured	

Maintenance Records, Modifications, Photo, or Receipt

_____

_____

_____

_____

_____

_____

Make	
Model Name/Number	
Serial Number	
Manufacturer/Importer	
Caliber	
Capacity	
Action	
Barrel Length	
Finish	
Stock/Fore-end	
Sights	
Scope	
Condition	

Other Characteristics, Special Marks & Accessories

_____

_____

_____

_____

_____

Date Purchased	
From (name/address or license no.)	
Price	

Date Sold	
To (name/address or license no.)	
Price	

Current/Replacement Value	
Insured	

Maintenance Records, Modifications, Photo, or Receipt

_____

_____

_____

_____

_____

_____

_____

Historical Timeline of Firearms
(1776–1840)

1776	American Revolution, where a flintlock rifled muzzleloader, known as the Pennsylvania Rifle, is used extensively. The long rifle was used by Daniel Boone in Kentucky, so it also became known as the Kentucky Rifle.
1777	The often lavishly decorated dueling pistol is officially standardized as a smoothbore flintlock with a 9- or 10-inch barrel and of a 1-inch bore, "carrying a ball of 48 to the pound."
1794	George Washington's Springfield Armory, established in 1777, begins manufacturing muskets for the U.S. military.

1805	The percussion-detonating principle is discovered (and patented two years later) by Scotsman Alexander Forsyth, the father of modern ignition. He found that potassium chlorate (or, fulminate primer material, a somewhat stable chemical compound) exploded when given a sharp blow by a gun's hammer; the strong flash ignited the main charge in the barrel. This is still the basis of today's primers.
1812	War of 1812, where Springfield Model 1795 and Harper's Ferry 1803 rifles are widely used. The same year, Swiss gunsmith Jean Samuel Pauly, the father of modern ammunition, invents a self-contained cartridge using the fulminate priming material, the first center-fire cartridge.

1815	Battle of Waterloo, where the infantry uses smoothbore flintlock muzzleloaders. These French muskets had also been used to support American troops during the Revolution.
1823	Jacob and Samuel Hawken design the Hawken rifle, a muzzleloader that becomes the favorite for frontiers folk hunting Plains game; shorter than the frontier long rifle, the 10-pound gun is owned by some of the time's most famous hunters, including Theodore Roosevelt and Daniel Boone.

1824	German inventor Johann Nikolaus von Dreyse creates a needle gun, based on Pauly's designs, that will become a mainstay of the Prussian army. The breech-loading rifle uses a needle that penetrates a paper cartridge before igniting a black-powder charge, which fires the bullet.
1825	Percussion-cap guns, which can reliably fire in any weather, are in general use.
1835	Samuel Colt develops the Colt revolver, the first multi-shot, revolving firearm (where the cylinders rotate around a fixed barrel), making them reliable and accurate. Because they're mass produced, they become affordable.
1840	Guns begin to use pin-fire cartridges, developed and patented by Casimir Lefaucheux in 1835, as a metallic head on a cardboard or paper cartridge body with a percussion cap on the outside of the case head; once the firing pin was struck, it would detonate the primer on the inside.

Make	
Model Name/Number	
Serial Number	
Manufacturer/Importer	
Caliber	
Capacity	
Action	
Barrel Length	
Finish	
Stock/Fore-end	
Sights	
Scope	
Condition	

Other Characteristics, Special Marks & Accessories

_____

_____

_____

_____

_____

Date Purchased	
From (name/address or license no.)	
Price	

Date Sold	
To (name/address or license no.)	
Price	

Current/Replacement Value	
Insured	

Maintenance Records, Modifications, Photo, or Receipt

_____

_____

_____

_____

_____

_____

Make	
Model Name/Number	
Serial Number	
Manufacturer/Importer	
Caliber	
Capacity	
Action	
Barrel Length	
Finish	
Stock/Fore-end	
Sights	
Scope	
Condition	

Other Characteristics, Special Marks & Accessories

_____

_____

_____

_____

_____

Date Purchased	
From (name/address or license no.)	
Price	

Date Sold	
To (name/address or license no.)	
Price	

Current/Replacement Value	
Insured	

Maintenance Records, Modifications, Photo, or Receipt

_____

_____

_____

_____

_____

_____

_____

Make	
Model Name/Number	
Serial Number	
Manufacturer/Importer	
Caliber	
Capacity	
Action	
Barrel Length	
Finish	
Stock/Fore-end	
Sights	
Scope	
Condition	

Other Characteristics, Special Marks & Accessories

_____

_____

_____

_____

_____

Date Purchased	
From (name/address or license no.)	
Price	

Date Sold	
To (name/address or license no.)	
Price	

Current/Replacement Value	
Insured	

Maintenance Records, Modifications, Photo, or Receipt

_____

_____

_____

_____

_____

_____

_____

Make	
Model Name/Number	
Serial Number	
Manufacturer/Importer	
Caliber	
Capacity	
Action	
Barrel Length	
Finish	
Stock/Fore-end	
Sights	
Scope	
Condition	

Other Characteristics, Special Marks & Accessories

_____

_____

_____

_____

_____

ACQUISITION & DISPOSITION

Date Purchased	
From (name/address or license no.)	
Price	

Date Sold	
To (name/address or license no.)	
Price	

Current/Replacement Value	
Insured	

Maintenance Records, Modifications, Photo, or Receipt

_____

_____

_____

_____

_____

_____

_____

Shotguns

A weapon designed or redesigned, made or remade, and intended to be fired from the shoulder, and designed or redesigned and made or remade to use the energy of an explosive to fire through a smooth bore either a number of ball shot or a single projectile for each single pull of the trigger.

~ 26 U.S.C. Chapter 53 §5845(d)

Make	
Model Name/Number	
Serial Number	
Manufacturer/Importer	
Gauge & Type	
Capacity	
Action	
Choke(s)	
Barrel Length & Type	
Finish	
Stock/Fore-end	
Sights	
Condition	

Other Characteristics, Special Marks & Accessories

_____

_____

_____

_____

_____

Date Purchased	
From (name/address or license no.)	
Price	

Date Sold	
To (name/address or license no.)	
Price	

Current/Replacement Value	
Insured	

Maintenance Records, Modifications, Photo, or Receipt

_____

_____

_____

_____

_____

_____

Make	
Model Name/Number	
Serial Number	
Manufacturer/Importer	
Gauge & Type	
Capacity	
Action	
Choke(s)	
Barrel Length & Type	
Finish	
Stock/Fore-end	
Sights	
Condition	

Other Characteristics, Special Marks & Accessories

_____

_____

_____

_____

_____

Date Purchased	
From (name/address or license no.)	
Price	

Date Sold	
To (name/address or license no.)	
Price	

Current/Replacement Value	
Insured	

Maintenance Records, Modifications, Photo, or Receipt

_____

_____

_____

_____

_____

_____

_____

Make	
Model Name/Number	
Serial Number	
Manufacturer/Importer	
Gauge & Type	
Capacity	
Action	
Choke(s)	
Barrel Length & Type	
Finish	
Stock/Fore-end	
Sights	
Condition	

Other Characteristics, Special Marks & Accessories

_____

_____

_____

_____

_____

Date Purchased	
From (name/address or license no.)	
Price	

Date Sold	
To (name/address or license no.)	
Price	

Current/Replacement Value	
Insured	

Maintenance Records, Modifications, Photo, or Receipt

_____

_____

_____

_____

_____

_____

_____

Make	
Model Name/Number	
Serial Number	
Manufacturer/Importer	
Gauge & Type	
Capacity	
Action	
Choke(s)	
Barrel Length & Type	
Finish	
Stock/Fore-end	
Sights	
Condition	

Other Characteristics, Special Marks & Accessories

_____

_____

_____

_____

_____

Date Purchased	
From (name/address or license no.)	
Price	

Date Sold	
To (name/address or license no.)	
Price	

Current/Replacement Value	
Insured	

Maintenance Records, Modifications, Photo, or Receipt

_____

_____

_____

_____

_____

_____

_____

Popular Firearms of Western Gunslingers

William H. Bonney, better known as Billy the Kid, was a gunslinger and outlaw who shot and stole his way through the Western Territories with whatever weapons he could get his hands on. The gun that took him down in 1881, however, wielded by Sheriff Pat Garrett, was a .44-40 caliber Colt Army revolver. Ironically, the gun had been confiscated from a member of the Kid's own gang the year before.

Robbers of banks, stagecoaches, and trains, Jesse James and his brother Frank favored Smith & Wesson pistols. While Jesse undoubtedly used the Colt .45 Peacemaker after its appearance in 1873, and occasionally a Remington or Winchester, it was the Smith & Wesson Schofield that could be used one-handed—and Jesse was known to carry two.

Frontiersman James "Wild Bill" Hickock
was a gunfighter, gambler, and lawman oft-
considered a "hero of the West." His favored
firearm was the Colt .36-caliber, six-shot, 1851
Navy revolver, which also happened to be the
most popular firearm among the military,
peace officers, and civilians. He carried two,
with handsome ivory grips, referring to them
as "equalizers" (to make things "equal as
possible").

Hickock's lifelong friend, William "Buffalo Bill" Cody,
was a rider on the Pony Express, a Union scout
during the Civil War, and one of the world's first
global celebrities, owing to his Wild West Show. He
earned his moniker when he began hunting buffalo
to feed the Union Pacific Railroad work crews in
1867—killing more than 4,200 animals with an Allin
Conversion .50–70 caliber Springfield rifle, which he
named "Lucretia Borgia."

Make	
Model Name/Number	
Serial Number	
Manufacturer/Importer	
Gauge & Type	
Capacity	
Action	
Choke(s)	
Barrel Length & Type	
Finish	
Stock/Fore-end	
Sights	
Condition	

Other Characteristics, Special Marks & Accessories

_____

_____

_____

_____

_____

ACQUISITION & DISPOSITION

Date Purchased	
From (name/address or license no.)	
Price	

Date Sold	
To (name/address or license no.)	
Price	

Current/Replacement Value	
Insured	

Maintenance Records, Modifications, Photo, or Receipt

_____

_____

_____

_____

_____

_____

_____

Make	
Model Name/Number	
Serial Number	
Manufacturer/Importer	
Gauge & Type	
Capacity	
Action	
Choke(s)	
Barrel Length & Type	
Finish	
Stock/Fore-end	
Sights	
Condition	

Other Characteristics, Special Marks & Accessories

_____

_____

_____

_____

_____

Date Purchased	
From (name/address or license no.)	
Price	

Date Sold	
To (name/address or license no.)	
Price	

Current/Replacement Value	
Insured	

Maintenance Records, Modifications, Photo, or Receipt

_____

_____

_____

_____

_____

_____

_____

Make	
Model Name/Number	
Serial Number	
Manufacturer/Importer	
Gauge & Type	
Capacity	
Action	
Choke(s)	
Barrel Length & Type	
Finish	
Stock/Fore-end	
Sights	
Condition	

Other Characteristics, Special Marks & Accessories

_____

_____

_____

_____

_____

Date Purchased	
From (name/address or license no.)	
Price	

Date Sold	
To (name/address or license no.)	
Price	

Current/Replacement Value	
Insured	

Maintenance Records, Modifications, Photo, or Receipt

_____

_____

_____

_____

_____

_____

_____

Make	
Model Name/Number	
Serial Number	
Manufacturer/Importer	
Gauge & Type	
Capacity	
Action	
Choke(s)	
Barrel Length & Type	
Finish	
Stock/Fore-end	
Sights	
Condition	

Other Characteristics, Special Marks & Accessories

_____

_____

_____

_____

_____

Date Purchased	
From (name/address or license no.)	
Price	

Date Sold	
To (name/address or license no.)	
Price	

Current/Replacement Value	
Insured	

Maintenance Records, Modifications, Photo, or Receipt

_____

_____

_____

_____

_____

_____

_____

Historical Timeline of Firearms
(1842–1869)

| 1842 | Great Britain and the United States begin to manufacture military firearms incorporating the percussion system. |

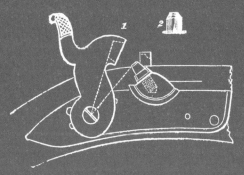

| 1845 | The first full rim-fire cartridge is developed by Frenchman Louis-Nicolas Flobert. |

| 1850 | True shotguns (smoothbore long barrels) are now in common use. |

| 1851 | British gunsmith Robert Adams patents the first one-piece percussion revolver, with "a self-cocking lockwork," where the trigger both cocks the hammer and fires the gun. |

| 1854 | Crimean War, the last war to use only muzzle-loaded guns. That same year, Lt. Frederick Beaumont improves upon Adams's lockwork, creating what would be called a "double action" revolver today. |

| 1857 | Horace Smith and Daniel B. Wesson produce a popular .22 caliber revolver, the Model 1, that uses rimfire cartridges. |

| 1860 | The Spencer repeating carbine is patented, using cartridges that could fire 7 shots in 15 seconds. |

| 1861 | American Civil War, using both breech- and muzzle-loaded guns. Soldiers on both sides privately keep Smith & Wesson Model 1s for self-defense. Breech-loaded guns are now in common use, where the ammunition is loaded in the rear (breech) of the barrel, rather than the front (muzzle). |

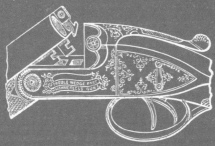

| 1862 | Richard Jordan Gatling invents the Gatling gun, a multi-barreled rotating gun operated by a hand crank that could fire up to 200 rounds per minute. |

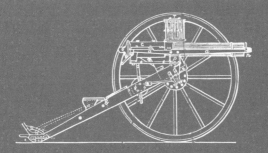

| 1863 | Abraham Lincoln test-fires a Spencer, and his approval leads to it becoming the principal repeating gun of the Civil War. |

| 1869 | The center-fire cartridge is invented. |

Make	
Model Name/Number	
Serial Number	
Manufacturer/Importer	
Gauge & Type	
Capacity	
Action	
Choke(s)	
Barrel Length & Type	
Finish	
Stock/Fore-end	
Sights	
Condition	

Other Characteristics, Special Marks & Accessories

_____

_____

_____

_____

_____

Date Purchased	
From (name/address or license no.)	
Price	

Date Sold	
To (name/address or license no.)	
Price	

Current/Replacement Value	
Insured	

Maintenance Records, Modifications, Photo, or Receipt

_____

_____

_____

_____

_____

_____

_____

Make	
Model Name/Number	
Serial Number	
Manufacturer/Importer	
Gauge & Type	
Capacity	
Action	
Choke(s)	
Barrel Length & Type	
Finish	
Stock/Fore-end	
Sights	
Condition	

Other Characteristics, Special Marks & Accessories

_____

_____

_____

_____

_____

Date Purchased	
From (name/address or license no.)	
Price	

Date Sold	
To (name/address or license no.)	
Price	

Current/Replacement Value	
Insured	

Maintenance Records, Modifications, Photo, or Receipt

_____

_____

_____

_____

_____

_____

_____

Make	
Model Name/Number	
Serial Number	
Manufacturer/Importer	
Gauge & Type	
Capacity	
Action	
Choke(s)	
Barrel Length & Type	
Finish	
Stock/Fore-end	
Sights	
Condition	

Other Characteristics, Special Marks & Accessories

_____

_____

_____

_____

_____

Date Purchased	
From (name/address or license no.)	
Price	

Date Sold	
To (name/address or license no.)	
Price	

Current/Replacement Value	
Insured	

Maintenance Records, Modifications, Photo, or Receipt

_____

_____

_____

_____

_____

_____

_____

Make	
Model Name/Number	
Serial Number	
Manufacturer/Importer	
Gauge & Type	
Capacity	
Action	
Choke(s)	
Barrel Length & Type	
Finish	
Stock/Fore-end	
Sights	
Condition	

Other Characteristics, Special Marks & Accessories

_____

_____

_____

_____

_____

Date Purchased	
From (name/address or license no.)	
Price	

Date Sold	
To (name/address or license no.)	
Price	

Current/Replacement Value	
Insured	

Maintenance Records, Modifications, Photo, or Receipt

_____

_____

_____

_____

_____

_____

_____

The Most Expensive Guns Ever Sold

Is it an investment, or is it art? A truly classic firearm can be both, as these winning bids reveal.

In 2018, a private collector won a Danish Sea Captain Colt Walker percussion revolver for $1.84 million. There were only 100 civilian Colt Walkers made, and very few are known to still exist. This particular model is the only known one that still has the original factory case and original sale documentation written by Sam Colt. Purchased by Danish sea captain Neils Hanson in New York City in 1847, it later survived the Nazi occupation of Denmark.

In 2002, Fort Ligonier in Pennsylvania paid $1.98 million at auction for a pair of pistols gifted to George Washinton by the Marquis de Lafayette during the Revolutionary War. When the Marquis visited Andew Jackson in 1826, he verified the pistols in Jackson's possession were the very same ones he had given to Washington. Made by Jacob Walster, they were later bequeathed to Lafayette's son, George Washington Lafayette.

In 2021, a private collector won an auction for the gun Pat Garrett used to kill Billy the Kid for $6.03 million. The Colt Single Action Army .44-40 caliber revolver with a walnut grip was taken off Billy Wilson, a member of Billy the Kid's gang, when Garrett arrested Wilson at Stinking Springs. Garrett took to carrying the gun himself, including on the fateful day, July 14, 1881, when he shot Billy the Kid in the chest.

> "Don't let yesterday use up too much of today."

Will Rogers

Make	
Model Name/Number	
Serial Number	
Manufacturer/Importer	
Gauge & Type	
Capacity	
Action	
Choke(s)	
Barrel Length & Type	
Finish	
Stock/Fore-end	
Sights	
Condition	

Other Characteristics, Special Marks & Accessories

_____

_____

_____

_____

_____

Date Purchased	
From (name/address or license no.)	
Price	

Date Sold	
To (name/address or license no.)	
Price	

Current/Replacement Value	
Insured	

Maintenance Records, Modifications, Photo, or Receipt

_____

_____

_____

_____

_____

_____

_____

Make	
Model Name/Number	
Serial Number	
Manufacturer/Importer	
Gauge & Type	
Capacity	
Action	
Choke(s)	
Barrel Length & Type	
Finish	
Stock/Fore-end	
Sights	
Condition	

Other Characteristics, Special Marks & Accessories

_____

_____

_____

_____

_____

Date Purchased	
From (name/address or license no.)	
Price	

Date Sold	
To (name/address or license no.)	
Price	

Current/Replacement Value	
Insured	

Maintenance Records, Modifications, Photo, or Receipt

_____

_____

_____

_____

_____

_____

_____

Make	
Model Name/Number	
Serial Number	
Manufacturer/Importer	
Gauge & Type	
Capacity	
Action	
Choke(s)	
Barrel Length & Type	
Finish	
Stock/Fore-end	
Sights	
Condition	

Other Characteristics, Special Marks & Accessories

_____

_____

_____

_____

_____

Date Purchased	
From (name/address or license no.)	
Price	

Date Sold	
To (name/address or license no.)	
Price	

Current/Replacement Value	
Insured	

Maintenance Records, Modifications, Photo, or Receipt

_____

_____

_____

_____

_____

_____

_____

Make	
Model Name/Number	
Serial Number	
Manufacturer/Importer	
Gauge & Type	
Capacity	
Action	
Choke(s)	
Barrel Length & Type	
Finish	
Stock/Fore-end	
Sights	
Condition	

Other Characteristics, Special Marks & Accessories

_____

_____

_____

_____

_____

Date Purchased	
From (name/address or license no.)	
Price	

Date Sold	
To (name/address or license no.)	
Price	

Current/Replacement Value	
Insured	

Maintenance Records, Modifications, Photo, or Receipt

_____

_____

_____

_____

_____

_____

Historical Timeline of Firearms
(1870–1900)

1870	Franco-Prussian War, where breech-loaded guns, particularly the Fusil modèle 1866 (Chassepot) are predominantly used by the French.
1871	Colt designs the first metallic-cartridge revolver.
1873	The Winchester rifle is introduced; produced in such great numbers at an affordable price, it becomes the generic rifle, though it also comes to be known as "the gun that won the West." Colt also introduces the Peacemaker, a Single Action revolver, which becomes popular among the military and gunslingers alike.
1877	Colt manufactures their first effective double-action revolver, the M1877. Offered in three calibers, they become known as the Thunderer, the Lightning, and the Rainmaker.

1879	James Paris Lee patents the Lee box magazine, which holds rounds stacked vertically. That same year, John Moses Browning patents a self-cocking single-shot rifle, which he and his brother sell to the Winchester Repeating Arms Company.

| 1883 | American engineer Hiram Maxim devises (and patents two years later) the first automatic machine gun. Dubbed the "Devil's Paintbrush," it uses the recoil to eject spent cartridges and load fresh ones from an ammunition belt at 500 rounds per minute. |

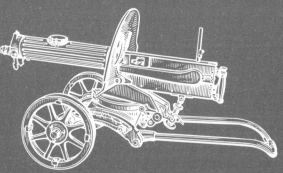

| 1887 | Winchester comes out with their first successful repeating shotguns with a lever action. |

| 1891 | The first automatic handgun is invented by Austrian Archduke Karl Salvator and Count Georg Von Dormus. |

| 1893 | Hugo Borchardt develops a pistol that is the first semiautomatic handgun with a separate magazine in the grip. The same year, Winchester introduces a pump-action shotgun designed by Browning. |

| 1898 | Borchardt's assistant, Georg Luger, adapts Borchardt's design and creates the Parabellum pistol to replace single-action revolvers. |

| 1900 | Automatics—including Colt, Browning, Luger, and Mauser—are firmly established by the turn of the century. The Contemporary period of firearms begins. |

Make	
Model Name/Number	
Serial Number	
Manufacturer/Importer	
Gauge & Type	
Capacity	
Action	
Choke(s)	
Barrel Length & Type	
Finish	
Stock/Fore-end	
Sights	
Condition	

Other Characteristics, Special Marks & Accessories

_____

_____

_____

_____

_____

Date Purchased	
From (name/address or license no.)	
Price	

Date Sold	
To (name/address or license no.)	
Price	

Current/Replacement Value	
Insured	

Maintenance Records, Modifications, Photo, or Receipt

_____

_____

_____

_____

_____

_____

_____

Make	
Model Name/Number	
Serial Number	
Manufacturer/Importer	
Gauge & Type	
Capacity	
Action	
Choke(s)	
Barrel Length & Type	
Finish	
Stock/Fore-end	
Sights	
Condition	

Other Characteristics, Special Marks & Accessories

_____

_____

_____

_____

_____

Date Purchased	
From (name/address or license no.)	
Price	

Date Sold	
To (name/address or license no.)	
Price	

Current/Replacement Value	
Insured	

Maintenance Records, Modifications, Photo, or Receipt

_____

_____

_____

_____

_____

_____

_____

Make	
Model Name/Number	
Serial Number	
Manufacturer/Importer	
Gauge & Type	
Capacity	
Action	
Choke(s)	
Barrel Length & Type	
Finish	
Stock/Fore-end	
Sights	
Condition	

Other Characteristics, Special Marks & Accessories

_____

_____

_____

_____

_____

Date Purchased	
From (name/address or license no.)	
Price	

Date Sold	
To (name/address or license no.)	
Price	

Current/Replacement Value	
Insured	

Maintenance Records, Modifications, Photo, or Receipt

_____

_____

_____

_____

_____

_____

_____

Make	
Model Name/Number	
Serial Number	
Manufacturer/Importer	
Gauge & Type	
Capacity	
Action	
Choke(s)	
Barrel Length & Type	
Finish	
Stock/Fore-end	
Sights	
Condition	

Other Characteristics, Special Marks & Accessories

_____

_____

_____

_____

_____

Date Purchased	
From (name/address or license no.)	
Price	

Date Sold	
To (name/address or license no.)	
Price	

Current/Replacement Value	
Insured	

Maintenance Records, Modifications, Photo, or Receipt

_____

_____

_____

_____

_____

_____

_____

Handguns

Any firearm which has a short stock and is designed
to be held and fired by the use of a single hand.

~ ATF 27 CFR §478.11

Make	
Model Name/Number	
Serial Number	
Manufacturer/Importer	
Caliber	
Capacity	
Action	
Barrel Length	
Grips	
Finish	
Sights	
Scope	
Condition	

Other Characteristics, Special Marks & Accessories

_____

_____

_____

_____

_____

Date Purchased	
From (name/address or license no.)	
Price	

Date Sold	
To (name/address or license no.)	
Price	

Current/Replacement Value	
Insured	

Maintenance Records, Modifications, Photo, or Receipt

_____

_____

_____

_____

_____

_____

_____

Make	
Model Name/Number	
Serial Number	
Manufacturer/Importer	
Caliber	
Capacity	
Action	
Barrel Length	
Grips	
Finish	
Sights	
Scope	
Condition	

Other Characteristics, Special Marks & Accessories

_____

_____

_____

_____

_____

ACQUISITION & DISPOSITION

Date Purchased	
From (name/address or license no.)	
Price	

Date Sold	
To (name/address or license no.)	
Price	

Current/Replacement Value	
Insured	

Maintenance Records, Modifications, Photo, or Receipt

_____

_____

_____

_____

_____

_____

_____

Make	
Model Name/Number	
Serial Number	
Manufacturer/Importer	
Caliber	
Capacity	
Action	
Barrel Length	
Grips	
Finish	
Sights	
Scope	
Condition	

Other Characteristics, Special Marks & Accessories

_____

_____

_____

_____

_____

Date Purchased	
From (name/address or license no.)	
Price	

Date Sold	
To (name/address or license no.)	
Price	

Current/Replacement Value	
Insured	

Maintenance Records, Modifications, Photo, or Receipt

_____

_____

_____

_____

_____

_____

Make	
Model Name/Number	
Serial Number	
Manufacturer/Importer	
Caliber	
Capacity	
Action	
Barrel Length	
Grips	
Finish	
Sights	
Scope	
Condition	

Other Characteristics, Special Marks & Accessories

_____

_____

_____

_____

_____

Date Purchased	
From (name/address or license no.)	
Price	

Date Sold	
To (name/address or license no.)	
Price	

Current/Replacement Value	
Insured	

Maintenance Records, Modifications, Photo, or Receipt

_____

_____

_____

_____

_____

_____

Popular Firearms of Western Gunslingers

Dubbed "Little Sure Shot" as part of Buffalo Bill's Wild West Extravaganza, Annie Oakley had a reputation for incredible marksmanship. She owned many guns, including a Winchester 1873 .44-40 caliber smoothbore rifle given her by Bill Cody, but she preferred plain guns with open sights. Her collection included Parkers, Remingtons, Smith & Wessons, and Colts, but after British gun maker Charles Lancaster custom-made a 12-bore double-barreled hammerless shotgun for her size in 1888, Oakley specified that her rifles and shotguns be built the same.

As leader of the "Wild Bunch," Robert Parker, better known as Butch Cassidy, was a bank and train robber. In 1899, in an effort to gain amnesty, Cassidy turned over his 1873 Winchester .44–40 carbine and his holstered Colt .45 Single Action Army revolver with nickel finish and eagles on the grips (serial #158402—the most-documented Cassidy gun in existence). The governor of Utah, erroneously believing that Cassidy had committed murder, denied his request.

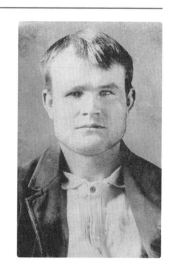

Belle Starr, the self-fashioned "bandit queen," was a notorious outlaw and friend of the James brothers. Born Myra Shirley, she was often depicted either as elegantly dressed in velvet and feathers, or in buckskins and boots with a man's Stetson. In either case, she toted a Colt .45. She organized robberies, harbored criminals, and was convicted of horse theft, but she was perhaps best known for her death: shot in the back while riding her horse, a crime that went unsolved.

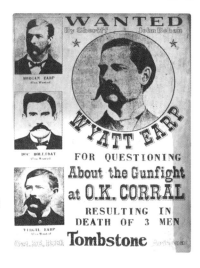

John Henry "Doc" Holliday was a gentleman gunfighter and friend of Wyatt Earp. He gave up dentistry for gambling and, with a trail of crimes across several states, became deputized in Tombstone, Arizona, before the famous 1881 gunfight at the O.K. Corral. While Doc's first shot was from a shotgun, the gun had been handed to him by Virgil Earp and he dropped it after that single shot. Instead, Holliday's weapon of choice was an 1851 Colt Navy Peacemaker; he later carried a nickel-plated .41 caliber Colt Thunder or a .38 caliber Colt Lightning (though it is unconfirmed whether he carried one in a shoulder holster and another on his hip, as has been portrayed).

Make	
Model Name/Number	
Serial Number	
Manufacturer/Importer	
Caliber	
Capacity	
Action	
Barrel Length	
Grips	
Finish	
Sights	
Scope	
Condition	

Other Characteristics, Special Marks & Accessories

_____

_____

_____

_____

_____

Date Purchased	
From (name/address or license no.)	
Price	

Date Sold	
To (name/address or license no.)	
Price	

Current/Replacement Value	
Insured	

Maintenance Records, Modifications, Photo, or Receipt

_____

_____

_____

_____

_____

_____

_____

Make	
Model Name/Number	
Serial Number	
Manufacturer/Importer	
Caliber	
Capacity	
Action	
Barrel Length	
Grips	
Finish	
Sights	
Scope	
Condition	

Other Characteristics, Special Marks & Accessories

_____

_____

_____

_____

_____

Date Purchased	
From (name/address or license no.)	
Price	

Date Sold	
To (name/address or license no.)	
Price	

Current/Replacement Value	
Insured	

Maintenance Records, Modifications, Photo, or Receipt

_____

_____

_____

_____

_____

_____

_____

Make	
Model Name/Number	
Serial Number	
Manufacturer/Importer	
Caliber	
Capacity	
Action	
Barrel Length	
Grips	
Finish	
Sights	
Scope	
Condition	

Other Characteristics, Special Marks & Accessories

_____

_____

_____

_____

_____

Date Purchased	
From (name/address or license no.)	
Price	

Date Sold	
To (name/address or license no.)	
Price	

Current/Replacement Value	
Insured	

Maintenance Records, Modifications, Photo, or Receipt

_____

_____

_____

_____

_____

_____

Make	
Model Name/Number	
Serial Number	
Manufacturer/Importer	
Caliber	
Capacity	
Action	
Barrel Length	
Grips	
Finish	
Sights	
Scope	
Condition	

Other Characteristics, Special Marks & Accessories

_____

_____

_____

_____

_____

Date Purchased	
From (name/address or license no.)	
Price	

Date Sold	
To (name/address or license no.)	
Price	

Current/Replacement Value	
Insured	

Maintenance Records, Modifications, Photo, or Receipt

_____

_____

_____

_____

_____

_____

_____

Modern Timeline of Firearms
(1900–1947)

1900

While the telescopic lens was nothing new, Irish optical designer Howard Grubb develops the reflective sight, or "reflex sight," for small arms. It allows for sighting with both eyes open.

1911

Browning's semiautomatic .45-caliber handgun, the M1911, using the short-recoil principle, is formally adopted by the U.S. Army. Widely copied throughout the 20th century (and later improved to the M1911A1), it becomes the standard-issue sidearm for the U.S. Armed Forces, appearing in WWI, WWII, Korea, and Vietnam.

1917

Maxim's machine gun, and later a Browning model, is predominantly used by U.S. forces in World War I; German forces use their own version of the weapon, the MG 08/15. The firepower on both sides leads to the development of trench warfare.

1918

John Thompson develops the submachine gun, a more lightweight and portable machine gun that is fully automatic, firing about 800 rounds per minute. Developed too late for much use in WWI, the "Tommy gun" comes to be the weapon of choice during Prohibition and later in WWII.

1928

John Garand, a Springfield Armory engineer and notable marksman, begins development of the .30-caliber M1 semiautomatic rifle, eventually described by General George S. Patton as "the greatest battle implement ever devised." It later becomes standard issue in WWII, known for automatically ejecting the clip when the last round is spent, allowing for the quicker insertion of another loaded clip.

1929	The St. Valentine's Day Massacre occurs in Chicago on February 14. The crime scene becomes one of the first times forensic ballistics is used; in this case, recovered bullets matched two Tommy guns of one of Al Capone's hitmen.
1935	Smith & Wesson unveils the .357 Magnum revolver with a longer barrel than the .38 Special and more firepower. Though the U.S. was in the midst of the Great Depression, Smith & Wesson charges a premium for the gun with a polished blue finish with customer's choice of sites, barrel length, and ammo. FBI director J. Edgar Hoover receives the first one on April 8.
1941	The U.S. enters WWII. The troops use Browning automatic rifles (BARs) and machine guns, the M1 Garand semiautomatic rifle, and American-made M3 .45-caliber submachine guns (by the end of 1942).
1942	Hugo Schmeisser develops a prototype of what would later be the basis for the AK-47. During WWII, Nazi Germany distributes Schmeisser's Sturmgewehr 44 to its soldiers, in addition to the Karabiner 98k Mauser. The StG 44 could shoot in semiautomatic and full-auto modes and its magazine could carry 30 rounds.
1947	Mikhail Kalashnikov develops the AK-47 for the Soviet military. At 10 pounds, it is a lighter-weight rapid-fire weapon with a short barrel and a banana-shaped magazine. (AK stands for Avtomat Kalashnikova, or "the Automatic by Kalashnikov.") It is gas operated and can fire up to 600 rounds a minute.

Make	
Model Name/Number	
Serial Number	
Manufacturer/Importer	
Caliber	
Capacity	
Action	
Barrel Length	
Grips	
Finish	
Sights	
Scope	
Condition	

Other Characteristics, Special Marks & Accessories

_____

_____

_____

_____

_____

Date Purchased	
From (name/address or license no.)	
Price	

Date Sold	
To (name/address or license no.)	
Price	

Current/Replacement Value	
Insured	

Maintenance Records, Modifications, Photo, or Receipt

_____

_____

_____

_____

_____

_____

_____

Make	
Model Name/Number	
Serial Number	
Manufacturer/Importer	
Caliber	
Capacity	
Action	
Barrel Length	
Grips	
Finish	
Sights	
Scope	
Condition	

Other Characteristics, Special Marks & Accessories

_____

_____

_____

_____

_____

Date Purchased	
From (name/address or license no.)	
Price	

Date Sold	
To (name/address or license no.)	
Price	

Current/Replacement Value	
Insured	

Maintenance Records, Modifications, Photo, or Receipt

_____

_____

_____

_____

_____

_____

_____

Make	
Model Name/Number	
Serial Number	
Manufacturer/Importer	
Caliber	
Capacity	
Action	
Barrel Length	
Grips	
Finish	
Sights	
Scope	
Condition	

Other Characteristics, Special Marks & Accessories

_____

_____

_____

_____

_____

Date Purchased	
From (name/address or license no.)	
Price	

Date Sold	
To (name/address or license no.)	
Price	

Current/Replacement Value	
Insured	

Maintenance Records, Modifications, Photo, or Receipt

_____

_____

_____

_____

_____

_____

_____

Make	
Model Name/Number	
Serial Number	
Manufacturer/Importer	
Caliber	
Capacity	
Action	
Barrel Length	
Grips	
Finish	
Sights	
Scope	
Condition	

Other Characteristics, Special Marks & Accessories

_____

_____

_____

_____

_____

Date Purchased	
From (name/address or license no.)	
Price	

Date Sold	
To (name/address or license no.)	
Price	

Current/Replacement Value	
Insured	

Maintenance Records, Modifications, Photo, or Receipt

_____

_____

_____

_____

_____

_____

The Hamilton-Burr Dueling Pistols

Thanks to U.S. History class or the Broadway musical (or both), you probably already know that Aaron Burr shot and killed Alexander Hamilton in a duel. However, it's not common knowledge what weapons were used on that fateful day. The .56-caliber smoothbore duelers, purchased by Hamilton's brother-in-law, were made by London gunsmith Robert Wogdon. They had octagonal barrels, bead front sights and notch rear, and checkered stocks. They were just a hair over the .50-caliber "limit" set for dueling pistols, which made these guns a little more deadly. It's inconclusive who shot first on that morning of July 11, 1804, but Hamilton died the next day from a gunshot wound to the stomach, taking Burr's public image with him.

Though dueling was a cultural fixture, it was banned in many states. Andew Jackson was a famed duelist; not even two years after Hamilton's death, he killed a lawyer named Charles Dickinson, before going on to becoming the nation's seventh president. By the time of the Civil War, dueling had begun its decline in the United States. To date, however, Washington state and Texas still allow "mutual combat" under specific circumstances: both parties have to consent, and it cannot result in serious bodily injury.

Aaron Burr

Alexander Hamilton

Make	
Model Name/Number	
Serial Number	
Manufacturer/Importer	
Caliber	
Capacity	
Action	
Barrel Length	
Grips	
Finish	
Sights	
Scope	
Condition	

Other Characteristics, Special Marks & Accessories

_____

_____

_____

_____

_____

Date Purchased	
From (name/address or license no.)	
Price	

Date Sold	
To (name/address or license no.)	
Price	

Current/Replacement Value	
Insured	

Maintenance Records, Modifications, Photo, or Receipt

_____

_____

_____

_____

_____

_____

_____

Make	
Model Name/Number	
Serial Number	
Manufacturer/Importer	
Caliber	
Capacity	
Action	
Barrel Length	
Grips	
Finish	
Sights	
Scope	
Condition	

Other Characteristics, Special Marks & Accessories

_____

_____

_____

_____

_____

Date Purchased	
From (name/address or license no.)	
Price	

Date Sold	
To (name/address or license no.)	
Price	

Current/Replacement Value	
Insured	

Maintenance Records, Modifications, Photo, or Receipt

_____

_____

_____

_____

_____

_____

_____

Make	
Model Name/Number	
Serial Number	
Manufacturer/Importer	
Caliber	
Capacity	
Action	
Barrel Length	
Grips	
Finish	
Sights	
Scope	
Condition	

Other Characteristics, Special Marks & Accessories

_____

_____

_____

_____

_____

Date Purchased	
From (name/address or license no.)	
Price	

Date Sold	
To (name/address or license no.)	
Price	

Current/Replacement Value	
Insured	

Maintenance Records, Modifications, Photo, or Receipt

_____

_____

_____

_____

_____

_____

_____

Make	
Model Name/Number	
Serial Number	
Manufacturer/Importer	
Caliber	
Capacity	
Action	
Barrel Length	
Grips	
Finish	
Sights	
Scope	
Condition	

Other Characteristics, Special Marks & Accessories

_____

_____

_____

_____

_____

Date Purchased	
From (name/address or license no.)	
Price	

Date Sold	
To (name/address or license no.)	
Price	

Current/Replacement Value	
Insured	

Maintenance Records, Modifications, Photo, or Receipt

_____

_____

_____

_____

_____

_____

_____

Modern Timeline of Firearms
(1950–Today)

1950	Production of M1 Garands ramps up at the Springfield Armory in response to the Korean War. These became known as "Post-WWII Garands." Other weapons in use by the U.S. include M1 and M2 Carbines.
1951	Production begins on the 9 mm Uzi submachine gun, designed by Israeli officer Uziel Gal in the 1940s. Its low recoil allows it to be used with one hand.

1954	Armalite is established as a division of the Fairchild Engine and Airplane Corporation in Hollywood, California. All rifles, beginning with the AR-1, are designated AR, short for "Armalite Rifle."
1958	With turbulence mounting in Vietnam, the Springfield Armory begins production of the M14 rifle, with a gas-operated firing system that could switch between semiautomatic and fully automatic modes. It also has a cleaning kit in the butt-trap and attachments for M2 bayonet and M76 rifle grenade launcher.
1959	The AKM (Avtomat Kalashnikova Modernized), a revised, lighter AK-47, enters production. It becomes the most prevalent (and most copied) AK around the world. It can fire single shots or automatic shots at up to 700 rounds per minute. That same year, the AR-7 Explorer becomes the first commercial (civilian) rifle produced by Armalite, based off the Air Force–adopted AR-5 Survival Rifle.

1962

Defense Secretary Robert S. McNamara begins pushing the Pentagon to produce a new U.S. assault weapon, which becomes known as the M16, reaching troops by 1965. Like the AK-47, it is gas operated and can fire up to 700 rounds a minute, but because it is prone to corrosion and jamming, it is ultimately ineffective in Vietnam.

1963

Gaston Glock, an Austrian engineer and manufacturer of injection molding parts and components, founds GLOCK. Designed with minimal complexity, Glock's pistols are more reliable, durable, and easier to maintain; with three internal safeties, they also protect against accidental discharge.

1968

Women make their shooting debut at the XIX Olympic Games in Mexico City, competing in men's events as part of teams.

1985

The 1911 is retired as the official service pistol, replaced by the Beretta M9. With double the capacity as the 1911, the M9 also has an ambidextrous safety and magazine release so it can be used by left- or right-handed people.

TODAY

Variants of the AK and the M16 are the most commonly used weapons in 21st century warfare worldwide.

Make	
Model Name/Number	
Serial Number	
Manufacturer/Importer	
Caliber	
Capacity	
Action	
Barrel Length	
Grips	
Finish	
Sights	
Scope	
Condition	

Other Characteristics, Special Marks & Accessories

_____

_____

_____

_____

_____

Date Purchased	
From (name/address or license no.)	
Price	

Date Sold	
To (name/address or license no.)	
Price	

Current/Replacement Value	
Insured	

Maintenance Records, Modifications, Photo, or Receipt

_____

_____

_____

_____

_____

_____

_____

Make	
Model Name/Number	
Serial Number	
Manufacturer/Importer	
Caliber	
Capacity	
Action	
Barrel Length	
Grips	
Finish	
Sights	
Scope	
Condition	

Other Characteristics, Special Marks & Accessories

_____

_____

_____

_____

_____

Date Purchased	
From (name/address or license no.)	
Price	

Date Sold	
To (name/address or license no.)	
Price	

Current/Replacement Value	
Insured	

Maintenance Records, Modifications, Photo, or Receipt

_____

_____

_____

_____

_____

_____

_____

Make	
Model Name/Number	
Serial Number	
Manufacturer/Importer	
Caliber	
Capacity	
Action	
Barrel Length	
Grips	
Finish	
Sights	
Scope	
Condition	

Other Characteristics, Special Marks & Accessories

_____

_____

_____

_____

_____

Date Purchased	
From (name/address or license no.)	
Price	

Date Sold	
To (name/address or license no.)	
Price	

Current/Replacement Value	
Insured	

Maintenance Records, Modifications, Photo, or Receipt

_____

_____

_____

_____

_____

_____

_____

Make	
Model Name/Number	
Serial Number	
Manufacturer/Importer	
Caliber	
Capacity	
Action	
Barrel Length	
Grips	
Finish	
Sights	
Scope	
Condition	

Other Characteristics, Special Marks & Accessories

_____

_____

_____

_____

_____

Date Purchased	
From (name/address or license no.)	
Price	

Date Sold	
To (name/address or license no.)	
Price	

Current/Replacement Value	
Insured	

Maintenance Records, Modifications, Photo, or Receipt

_____

_____

_____

_____

_____

_____

_____

Quarto

© 2024 Quarto Publishing Group USA Inc.

This edition published in 2024 by Chartwell Books,
an imprint of The Quarto Group
142 West 36th Street, 4th Floor
New York, NY 10018 USA
T (212) 779-4972 F (212) 779-6058
www.Quarto.com

10 9 8 7 6 5 4 3 2 1

Chartwell titles are also available at discount for retail, wholesale, promotional, and bulk purchase. For details, contact the Special Sales Manager by email at specialsales@quarto.com or by mail at The Quarto Group, Attn: Special Sales Manager, 100 Cummings Center Suite 265D, Beverly, MA 01915, USA.

ISBN: 978-0-7858-4325-2

Publisher: Wendy Friedman
Senior Design Manager: Michael Caputo
Editor: J. F. Kushnier

All stock photos and design elements ©Shutterstock

Printed in China

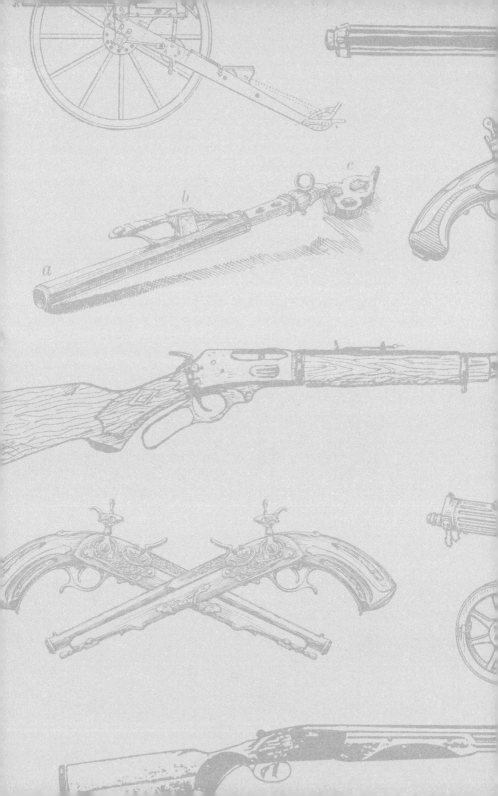